Letters
OF A WOMAN
HOMESTEADER

-PART ONE-

Elinore
Pruitt
Stewart

first published by
THE ATLANTIC
MONTHLY CO.
1913 – 1914

PUBLISHERS' NOTE

The writer of the
following letters is
a young woman who
lost her husband in
a railroad accident
and went to Denver
to seek support for
herself and her two-
year-old daughter,
Jerrine. Turning her
hand to the nearest
work, she went
out by the day as

house-cleaner and laundress. Later, seeking to better herself, she accepted employment as a housekeeper for a well-to-do Scotch cattle-man, Mr. Stewart, who had taken up a quarter-section in Wyoming. The letters, written through several years to a former employer in Denver, tell the story of her new life in the new country. They are genuine letters, and are printed as written, except for occasional omissions and the alteration of some of the names.

THE ARRIVAL AT BURNT FORK

Burnt Fork, Wyoming,
April 18, 1909.
Dear Mrs. Coney,—

Are you thinking I am lost, like the Babes in the Wood? Well, I am not and I'm sure the robins would have the time of their lives getting leaves to cover me out here. I am 'way up close to the Forest Reserve of Utah, within half a mile of the line, sixty miles from the railroad. I was twenty-four hours on the train and two days on the stage, and oh, those two days! The snow was just beginning to melt and the mud was about the worst I ever heard of.

The first stage we
tackled was just
about as rickety as
it could very well be
and I had to sit with
the driver, who was
a Mormon and so
handsome that I was
not a bit offended
when he insisted
on making love all
the way, especially
after he told me that
he was a widower
Mormon. But, of
course, as I had no

chaperone I looked very fierce (not that that was very difficult with the wind and mud as allies) and told him my actual opinion of Mormons in general and particular.

Meantime my new employer, Mr. Stewart, sat upon a stack of baggage and was dreadfully concerned about something he calls his "Tookie," but I am unable to tell you what that is. The road, being so muddy, was full of ruts and the stage acted as if it had the hiccoughs and made us all talk as though we were affected in the same way. Once Mr. Stewart asked me if I did not think it a "gey duir trip." I told him he could call it gay if he wanted to, but it didn't seem very hilarious to me. Every time the stage struck a rock or a rut Mr. Stewart would "hoot," until I began to wish we would come to a hollow tree or a hole in the ground so he could go in with the rest of the owls.

At last we "arriv," and everything is just lovely for me. I have a very, very comfortable situation and Mr. Stewart is absolutely no trouble, for as soon as he has his meals he retires to his room and plays on his bagpipe, only he calls it his "bugpeep." It is "The Campbells are Coming," without variations, at intervals all day long and from seven till eleven at night. Sometimes I wish

they would make
haste and get here.

There is a saddle
horse especially
for me and a little
shotgun with which
I am to kill sage
chickens. We are
between two trout
streams, so you can
think of me as being
happy when the snow
is through melting and
the water gets clear.
We have the finest

flock of Plymouth Rocks and get so many nice eggs. It sure seems fine to have all the cream I want after my town experiences. Jerrine is making good use of all the good things we are having. She rides the pony to water every day.

I have not filed on my land yet because the snow is fifteen feet deep on it, and I think I would rather see what I am getting, so will wait until summer. They have just three seasons here, winter and July and August. We are to plant our garden the last of May. When it is so I can get around I will see about land and find out all I can and tell you.

I think this letter

is about to reach thirty-secondly, so I will send you my sincerest love and quit tiring you. Please write me when you have time.

Sincerely yours,
Elinore Rupert.

FILING A CLAIM

May 24, 1909.
Dear, dear Mrs.
Coney,—

Well, I have filed on
my land and am now
a bloated landowner.
I waited a long time
to even see land in
the reserve, and the
snow is yet too deep,
so I thought that as
they have but three

months of summer and spring together and as I wanted the land for a ranch anyway, perhaps I had better stay in the valley. So I have filed adjoining Mr. Stewart and I am well pleased. I have a grove of twelve swamp pines on my place, and I am going to build my house there. I thought it would be very romantic to live on the peaks amid the whispering pines, but I reckon it would be powerfully uncomfortable also, and I guess my twelve can whisper enough for me; and a dandy thing is, I have all the nice snow-water I want; a small stream runs right through the center of my land and I am quite near wood.

A neighbor and his

daughter were going to Green River, the county-seat, and said I might go along, so I did, as I could file there as well as at the land office; and oh, that trip! I had more fun to the square inch than Mark Twain or Samantha Allen ever provoked. It took us a whole week to go and come. We camped out, of course, for in the whole sixty miles there was but one house, and going in that direction there is not a tree to be seen, nothing but sage, sand, and sheep. About noon the first day out we came near a sheep-wagon, and stalking along ahead of us was a lanky fellow, a herder, going home for dinner. Suddenly it seemed to me I should starve if I had to wait until we got where we had planned to stop for dinner, so I called out to the man, "Little Bo-Peep, have you anything to eat? If you have, we'd like to find it." And he answered, "As soon as I am able it shall be on the table, if you'll but trouble to get behind it." Shades of Shakespeare! Songs of David, the

Shepherd Poet! What do you think of us? Well, we got behind it, and a more delicious "it" I never tasted. Such coffee! And out of such a pot! I promised Bo-Peep that I would send him a crook with pink ribbons on it, but I suspect he thinks I am a crook without the ribbons.

The sagebrush is so

short in some places that it is not large enough to make a fire, so we had to drive until quite late before we camped that night. After driving all day over what seemed a level desert of sand, we came about sundown to a beautiful cañon, down which we had to drive for a couple of miles before we could cross. In the cañon the shadows had already fallen, but when we looked up we could see the last shafts of sunlight on the tops of the great bare buttes. Suddenly a great wolf started from somewhere and galloped along the edge of the cañon, outlined black and clear by the setting sun. His curiosity overcame him at last, so he sat down and waited to see what manner of beast we were. I reckon he was disappointed for he howled most dismally. I thought of Jack London's "The Wolf."

After we quitted the cañon I saw the most beautiful sight. It seemed as if we were driving through a golden haze. The violet shadows were creeping up

between the hills,
while away back of
us the snow-capped
peaks were catching
the sun's last rays.
On every side of us
stretched the poor,
hopeless desert,
the sage, grim and
determined to live in
spite of starvation,
and the great, bare,
desolate buttes.
The beautiful colors
turned to amber and
rose, and then to

the general tone,
dull gray. Then we
stopped to camp,
and such a scurrying
around to gather
brush for the fire
and to get supper!
Everything tasted
so good! Jerrine ate
like a man. Then we
raised the wagon
tongue and spread
the wagon sheet
over it and made
a bedroom for us
women. We made our

beds on the warm, soft sand and went to bed.

It was too beautiful a night to sleep, so I put my head out to look and to think. I saw the moon come up and hang for a while over the mountain as if it were discouraged with the prospect, and the big white stars flirted shamelessly with the hills. I saw

a coyote come
trotting along and I
felt sorry for him,
having to hunt food
in so barren a place,
but when presently
I heard the whirr of
wings I felt sorry for
the sage chickens
he had disturbed.
At length a cloud
came up and I went
to sleep, and next
morning was covered
several inches with
snow. It didn't hurt

us a bit, but while I was struggling with stubborn corsets and shoes I communed with myself, after the manner of prodigals, and said: "How much better that I were down in Denver, even at Mrs. Coney's, digging with a skewer into the corners seeking dirt which might be there, yea, even eating codfish, than that I should perish on this desert—of imagination." So I turned the current of my imagination and fancied that I was at home before the fireplace, and that the backlog was about to roll down. My fancy was in such good working trim that before I knew it I kicked the wagon wheel, and I certainly got as warm as the most "sot" Scientist that ever read Mrs. Eddy could possibly wish.

After two more such days I "arrived." When I went up to the office where I was to file, the door was open and the most taciturn old man sat before a desk. I hesitated at the door, but he never let on. I coughed, yet no sign but a deeper scowl. I stepped in and modestly kicked over a chair. He whirled around like I had shot him. "Well?" he interrogated. I said, "I am powerful glad of it. I was afraid you were sick, you looked in such pain." He looked at me a minute, then grinned and said he thought I was a book-agent. Fancy me, a fat, comfortable widow, trying to sell books!

Well, I filed and came home. If you will believe me, the Scot was glad to see me and didn't herald the Campbells for two hours after I got home. I'll tell you, it is mighty seldom any one's so much appreciated.

No, we have no rural delivery. It is two

miles to the office, but I go whenever I like. It is really the jolliest kind of fun to gallop down. We are sixty miles from the railroad, but when we want anything we send by the mail-carrier for it, only there is nothing to get.

I know this is an inexcusably long letter, but it is

snowing so hard and you know how I like to talk. I am sure Jerrine will enjoy the cards and we will be glad to get them. Many things that are a comfort to us out here came from dear Mrs. ——. Baby has the rabbit you gave her last Easter a year ago. In Denver I was afraid my baby would grow up devoid of imagination. Like all the kindergartners, she depended upon others to amuse her. I was very sorry about it, for my castles in Spain have been real homes to me. But there is no fear. She has a block of wood she found in the blacksmith shop which she calls her "dear baby." A spoke out of a wagon wheel is "little Margaret," and a barrel-stave is "bad little Johnny."

Well, I must quit writing before you vote me a nuisance. With lots of love to you,

Your sincere friend,
Elinore Rupert.

A BUSY, HAPPY SUMMER

September 11, 1909.
Dear Mrs. Coney,—

This has been for me the busiest, happiest summer I can remember. I have worked very hard, but it has been work that I really enjoy. Help of any kind is very hard to get here, and Mr. Stewart had been too confident of getting men, so that haying caught him with too few men to put up the hay. He had no man to run the mower and he couldn't run both the mower and the stacker, so you can fancy what a place he was in.

I don't know that I ever told you, but my

parents died within a year of each other and left six of us to shift for ourselves. Our people offered to take one here and there among them until we should all have a place, but we refused to be raised on the halves and so arranged to stay at Grandmother's and keep together. Well, we had no money to hire men to do our work, so had to learn to do it ourselves. Consequently I learned to do many things which girls more fortunately situated don't even know have to be done. Among the things I learned to do was the way to run a mowing-machine. It cost me many bitter tears because I got sunburned, and my hands were hard, rough, and stained with machine oil, and I used to wonder how any Prince Charming could overlook all that in any girl he came to. For all I had ever read of the Prince had to do with his "reverently kissing her lily-white hand," or doing some other fool trick with a hand as white as a snowflake. Well, when my Prince showed up he didn't lose much time in letting me know that "Barkis was willing," and I wrapped my hands in my old checked apron and took him up before he could catch his breath. Then there was no more mowing, and I almost forgot that I knew how until Mr. Stewart got into such a panic. If he put a man to mow, it kept them all idle at the stacker, and he just couldn't get enough men. I was afraid to tell him I could mow for fear he would forbid me to do so. But one morning, when he was chasing a last hope of help, I went down to the barn, took out the horses, and went to mowing. I had enough cut before he got back to show him I knew how, and as he came back manless he was delighted as well as surprised. I was glad because I really like to mow, and besides that, I am adding feathers to my cap in a surprising way. When you see me again you will think I am wearing a feather duster, but it is only that I have been said to have almost as much sense as a "mon," and that is an honor I never aspired to, even in my wildest dreams.

I have done most of my cooking at night, have milked seven cows every day, and have done all the hay-cutting, so you see I have been working. But I have found time to put up thirty pints of jelly and the same amount of jam for myself. I used wild fruits, gooseberries, currants, raspberries, and cherries. I have almost two gallons of the cherry butter, and I think it is delicious. I wish I could get some of it to you, I am sure you would like it.

We began haying July 5 and finished September 8. After working so hard and so steadily I decided on a day off, so yesterday I saddled the pony, took a few things I needed, and Jerrine and I fared forth. Baby can ride behind quite well. We got away by sunup and a glorious day we had. We followed a stream higher up into the mountains and the air was so keen and clear at first we had on our coats. There was a tang of sage and of pine in the air, and our horse was midside deep in rabbit-brush, a shrub just covered with flowers that look and smell like goldenrod. The blue distance promised many alluring adventures, so we went along singing and simply gulping in summer. Occasionally a bunch of sage chickens would fly up out of the sagebrush, or a jack rabbit would leap out. Once we saw a bunch of antelope gallop over a hill, but we were out just to be out, and game didn't tempt us. I started, though, to have just as good a time as possible, so I had a fish-hook in my knapsack.

Presently, about noon, we came to a

little dell where the grass was as soft and as green as a lawn. The creek kept right up against the hills on one side and there were groves of quaking asp and cottonwoods that made shade, and service-bushes and birches that shut off the ugly hills on the other side. We dismounted and prepared to noon.

We caught a few grasshoppers and I cut a birch pole for a rod. The trout are so beautiful now, their sides are so silvery, with dashes of old rose and orange, their speckles are so black, while their backs look as if they had been sprinkled with gold-dust. They bite so well that it doesn't require any especial skill or tackle to catch plenty for a meal in a few minutes.

In a little while I went back to where I had left my pony browsing, with eight beauties. We made a fire first, then I dressed my trout while it was burning down to a nice bed of coals. I had brought a frying-pan and a bottle of lard, salt, and buttered bread.

We gathered a few service-berries, our trout were soon browned, and with water, clear, and as cold as ice, we had a feast. The quaking aspens are beginning to turn yellow, but no leaves have fallen. Their shadows dimpled and twinkled over the grass like happy children. The sound of the dashing, roaring water kept inviting me to cast for trout, but I didn't want to carry them so far, so we rested until the sun was getting low and then started for home, with the song of the locusts in our ears warning us that the melancholy days are almost here. We would come up over the top of a hill into the glory of a beautiful sunset with its gorgeous colors, then down into the little valley already purpling with mysterious twilight. So on, until, just at dark, we rode into our corral and a mighty tired, sleepy little girl was powerfully glad to get home.

After I had mailed my other letter I was afraid that you would think me plumb bold about the little Bo-Peep, and was a heap sorrier than you can think. If you only knew the hardships these poor men endure. They go two together and sometimes it is months before they see another soul, and rarely ever a woman. I wouldn't act so free in town, but these men see people so seldom that they are awkward and embarrassed. I like to put them at ease, and it is to be done only by being kind of hail-fellow-well-met with them. So far not one has ever misunderstood me and I have been treated with every courtesy and kindness, so I am powerfully glad you understand. They really enjoy doing these little things like fixing our dinner, and if my poor company can add to any one's pleasure I am too glad.

Sincerely yours,
Elinore Rupert.

Mr. Stewart is going to put up my house for me in pay for my extra work.

I am ashamed of

my long letters to you, but I am such a murderer of language that I have to use it all to tell anything.

Please don't entirely forget me. Your letters mean so much to me and I will try to answer more promptly.

A CHARMING ADVENTURE AND ZEBULON PIKE

September 28, 1909.
Dear Mrs. Coney,—

Your second card just reached me and I am plumb glad because, although I answered your other, I was wishing I could write you, for I have had the most charming adventure.

It is the custom here for as many women as care to to go in a party over into Utah to Ashland (which is over a hundred miles away) after fruit. They usually go in September, and it takes a week to make the trip. They take wagons and camp out and of course have a good time, but, the greater part of the way, there isn't even the semblance of a road and it is merely a semblance anywhere. They came over to invite me to join them. I was of two minds—I wanted to go, but it seemed a little risky and a big chance for discomfort, since we would have to cross the Uinta Mountains, and a snowstorm likely any time. But I didn't like to refuse outright, so we left it to Mr. Stewart. His "Ye're nae gang" sounded powerful final, so the ladies departed in awed silence and I assumed a martyr-like air and acted like a very much abused woman, although he did only what I wanted him to do. At last, in sheer desperation he told me the "bairn canna stand the treep," and that was why he was so determined. I knew why, of course, but I continued to look abused lest he gets it into his head that he can boss me. After he had been reduced to the proper plane of humility and had explained and begged my pardon and had told me to consult only my own pleasure about going and coming and using his horses, only not to "expoose" the bairn, why, I forgave him and we were friends once more.

Next day all the men left for the roundup, to be gone a week. I knew I never could stand myself a whole week. In a little while the ladies came past on their

way to Ashland. They
were all laughing
and were so happy
that I really began
to wish I was one
of the number, but
they went their way
and I kept wanting
to go somewhere.
I got reckless and
determined to do
something real bad.
So I went down to
the barn and saddled
Robin Adair, placed
a pack on "Jeems

McGregor," then Jerrine and I left for a camping-out expedition.

It was nine o'clock when we started and we rode hard until about four, when I turned Robin loose, saddle and all, for I knew he would go home and some one would see him and put him into the pasture. We had gotten to where we couldn't ride anyway, so I put Jerrine on the pack and led "Jeems" for about two hours longer; then, as I had come to a good place to camp, we stopped.

While we had at least two good hours of daylight, it gets so cold here in the evening that fire is very necessary. We had been climbing higher into the mountains all day and had reached a level tableland where the grass was luxuriant and there was plenty of wood and water. I unpacked "Jeems" and staked him out, built a roaring fire, and made our bed in an angle of a sheer wall of rock where we would be protected against the wind. Then I put

some potatoes into
the embers, as Baby
and I are both fond
of roasted potatoes.
I started to a little
spring to get water
for my coffee when I
saw a couple of jack
rabbits playing, so
I went back for my
little shotgun. I shot
one of the rabbits,
so I felt very like
Leather-stocking
because I had killed
but one when I might

have gotten two. It was fat and young, and it was but the work of a moment to dress it and hang it up on a tree. Then I fried some slices of bacon, made myself a cup of coffee, and Jerrine and I sat on the ground and ate. Everything smelled and tasted so good! This air is so tonic that one gets delightfully hungry.

Afterward we watered and restaked "Jeems," I rolled some logs on to the fire, and then we sat and enjoyed the prospect.

The moon was so new that its light was very dim, but the stars were bright. Presently a long, quivering wail arose and was answered from a dozen hills. It seemed just the sound one ought to hear in such a place. When the howls ceased for a moment we could hear the subdued roar of the creek and the crooning of the wind in the pines. So we rather enjoyed the coyote chorus and were not afraid, because they don't attack people. Presently we crept under our Navajos and, being tired, were soon asleep.

I was awakened by a pebble striking my cheek. Something prowling on the bluff above us had dislodged it and it struck me. By my Waterbury it was four o'clock, so I arose and spitted my rabbit. The logs had left a big bed of coals, but some ends were still burning and had burned in such a manner that the heat would go both under and over my rabbit. So I put plenty of bacon grease over him and hung him up to roast. Then I went back to bed. I didn't want to start early because the air is too keen for comfort early in the morning.

The sun was just gilding the hilltops

when we arose. Everything, even the barrenness, was beautiful. We have had frosts, and the quaking aspens were a trembling field of gold as far up the stream as we could see. We were 'way up above them and could look far across the valley. We could see the silvery gold of the willows, the russet and bronze of the currants, and patches of cheerful green showed where the pines were. The splendor was relieved by a background of sober gray-green hills, but even on them gay streaks and patches of yellow showed where rabbit-brush grew. We washed our faces at the spring,—the grasses that grew around the edge and dipped into the water were loaded with ice,—our rabbit was done to a turn, so I made some delicious coffee, Jerrine got herself a can of water, and we breakfasted. Shortly afterwards we started again. We didn't know where we were going, but we were on our way.

That day was more

toilsome than the last, but a very happy one. The meadowlarks kept singing like they were glad to see us. But we were still climbing and soon got beyond the larks and sage chickens and up into the timber, where there are lots of grouse. We stopped to noon by a little lake, where I got two small squirrels

and a string of
trout. We had some
trout for dinner and
salted the rest with
the squirrels in an
empty can for future
use. I was anxious
to get a grouse and
kept close watch,
but was never quick
enough. Our progress
was now slower
and more difficult,
because in places we
could scarcely get
through the forest.

Fallen trees were everywhere and we had to avoid the branches, which was powerful hard to do. Besides, it was quite dusky among the trees long before night, but it was all so grand and awe-inspiring. Occasionally there was an opening through which we could see the snowy peaks, seemingly just beyond us, toward which we were headed. But when you get among such grandeur you get to feel how little you are and how foolish is human endeavor, except that which reunites us with the mighty force called God. I was plumb uncomfortable, because all my own efforts have always been just to make the best of everything and to take things as they come.

At last we came to an open side of the mountain where the trees were scattered. We were facing south and east, and the mountain we were on sheered away in a dangerous slant. Beyond us still greater wooded mountains blocked the way, and in the cañon between night had already fallen. I began to get scary. I could only think of bears and catamounts, so, as it was five o'clock, we decided to camp. The trees were immense. The lower branches came clear to the ground and grew so dense that any tree afforded a splendid shelter from the weather, but I was nervous and wanted one that would protect us against any possible attack. At last we found one growing in a crevice of what seemed to be a sheer wall of rock. Nothing could reach us on two sides, and in front two large trees had fallen so that I could make a log heap which would give us warmth and make us safe. So with rising spirits I unpacked and prepared for the night. I soon had a roaring fire up against the logs and, cutting away a few branches, let the heat into as snug a bedroom as any one could wish. The pine needles made as soft a carpet as the wealthiest could afford. Springs abound in the mountains, so water was plenty. I staked

"Jeems" quite near
so that the firelight
would frighten away
any wild thing that
tried to harm him.
Grass was very
plentiful, so when he
was made "comfy"
I made our bed and
fried our trout. The
branches had torn off
the bag in which I had
my bread, so it was
lost in the forest,
but who needs bread
when they have good,

mealy potatoes? In a short time we were eating like Lent was just over. We lost all the glory of the sunset except what we got by reflection, being on the side of the mountain we were, with the dense woods between. Big sullen clouds kept drifting over and a wind got lost in the trees that kept them rocking and groaning in a horrid way. But we were just as cozy as we could be and rest was as good as anything.

I wish you could once sleep on the kind of bed we enjoyed that night. It was both soft and firm, with the clean, spicy smell of the pine. The heat from our big fire came in and we were warm as toast. It was so good to stretch out and rest. I kept thinking how superior I was since I dared to take such an outing when so many poor women down in Denver were bent on making their twenty cents per hour in order that they could spare a quarter to go to the "show." I went to sleep with a powerfully self-satisfied feeling, but I awoke to realize that pride goeth before a fall.

I could hardly remember where I was when I awoke, and I could almost hear the silence. Not a tree moaned, not a branch seemed to stir. I arose and my head came in violent contact with a snag that was not there when I went to bed. I thought either I must have grown taller or the tree shorter during the night. As soon as I peered out, the mystery was explained.

Such a snowstorm I never saw! The snow had pressed the branches down lower, hence my bumped head. Our fire was burning merrily and the heat kept the snow from in front. I scrambled out and poked up the fire; then, as it was only five o'clock, I went back to bed. And then I began to think how many kinds of idiot I was. Here I was thirty or forty miles from home, in the mountains where no one goes in the winter and where I knew the snow got to be ten or fifteen feet deep. But I could never see the good of moping, so I got up and got breakfast while Baby put her shoes on. We had our squirrels and more baked potatoes and I had delicious black coffee.

After I had eaten I felt more hopeful. I knew Mr. Stewart would hunt for me if he knew I was lost. It was true, he wouldn't know which way to start, but I determined to rig up "Jeems" and turn him loose, for I knew he would go home and that he would leave a trail so that I could be found. I hated to do so, for I knew I should always have to be powerfully humble afterwards. Anyway it was still snowing, great, heavy flakes; they looked as large as dollars. I didn't want to start "Jeems" until the snow stopped because I wanted him to leave a clear trail. I had sixteen loads for my gun and I reasoned that I could likely kill enough food to last twice that many days by being careful what I shot at. It just kept snowing, so at last I decided to take a little hunt and provide for the day. I left Jerrine happy with the towel rolled into a baby, and went along the brow of the mountain for almost a mile, but the snow fell so thickly that I couldn't see far. Then I happened to look down into the cañon that lay east of us and saw smoke. I looked toward it a long time, but could make out nothing but smoke, but presently I heard a dog bark and I knew I was near a camp of some kind. I resolved to join them, so went back to break my own camp.

At last everything was ready and Jerrine and I both mounted. Of all the times! If you think there is much comfort, or even security, in riding a pack-horse in a snowstorm over mountains where there is no road, you are plumb wrong. Every once in a while a tree would unload its snow down our backs. "Jeems" kept stumbling and threatening to break our necks. At last we got down the mountain-side, where new danger confronted us,—we

might lose sight of
the smoke or ride into
a bog. But at last,
after what seemed
hours, we came into a
"clearing" with a small
log house and, what
is rare in Wyoming,
a fireplace. Three or
four hounds set up
their deep baying, and
I knew by the chimney
and the hounds that
it was the home of a
Southerner. A little
old man came bustling

out, chewing his tobacco so fast, and almost frantic about his suspenders, which it seemed he couldn't get adjusted.

As I rode up, he said, "Whither, friend?" I said "Hither." Then he asked, "Air you spying around for one of them dinged game wardens arter that deer I killed yisteddy?" I told him

I had never even seen a game warden and that I didn't know he had killed a deer. "Wall," he said, "air you spying around arter that gold mine I diskivered over on the west side of Baldy?" But after a while I convinced him that I was no more nor less than a foolish woman lost in the snow. Then he said, "Light, stranger, and look at your saddle." So I "lit" and looked, and then I asked him what part of the South he was from. He answered, "Yell County, by gum! The best place in the United States, or in the world, either." That was my introduction to Zebulon Pike Parker.

Only two "Johnny Rebs" could have

enjoyed each other's company as Zebulon Pike and myself did. He was so small and so old, but so cheerful and so sprightly, and a real Southerner! He had a big, open fireplace with backlogs and andirons. How I enjoyed it all! How we feasted on some of the deer killed "yisteddy," and real corn-pone baked in a skillet down on the hearth. He was so full of happy recollections and had a few that were not so happy! He is, in some way, a kinsman of Pike of Pike's Peak fame, and he came west "jist arter the wah" on some expedition and "jist stayed." He told me about his home life back in Yell County, and I feel that I know all the "young uns."

There was George Henry, his only brother; and there were Phœbe and "Mothie," whose real name is Martha; and poor little Mary Ann, whose death was described so feelingly that no one could keep back the tears. Lastly there was little Mandy, the baby and his favorite, but who, I am afraid, was a selfish little beast since she had to have her prunellas when all the rest of the "young uns" had to wear shoes that old Uncle Buck made out of rawhide. But then "her eyes were blue as morning-glories and her hair was jist like corn-silk, so yaller and fluffy." Bless his simple, honest heart! His own eyes are blue and kind, and his poor, thin little shoulders are so round that they almost meet in front. How he loved to talk of his boyhood days! I can almost see his father and George Henry as they marched away to the "wah" together, and the poor little mother's despair as she waited day after day for some word, that never came.

Poor little Mary Ann was drowned in the bayou, where she was trying to get water-lilies. She had wanted a white dress all her life and so, when she was dead, they took down the white cross-bar curtains and Mother made the little shroud by the light of a tallow dip. But, being made by hand, it took all the next day, too, so that they buried her by moonlight down back of the orchard under the big elm where the children had always had their swing. And they lined and covered her grave with big, fragrant water-lilies. As they lowered the poor little home-made coffin into the grave the mockingbirds began to sing and they sang all that dewy, moonlight night. Then little Mandy's wedding to Judge Carter's son Jim was described. She wore a "cream-colored poplin with a red rose throwed up in it," and the lace that was on Grandma's wedding dress. There were bowers of sweet Southern roses and honeysuckle and wistaria. Don't you know she was a dainty bride?

At last it came out
that he had not heard
from home since
he left it. "Don't
you ever write?" I
asked. "No, I am not
an eddicated man,
although I started
to school. Yes'm, I
started along of the
rest, but they told
me it was a Yankee
teacher and I was
'fraid, so when I

got most to the schoolhouse I hid in the bushes with my spelling-book, so that is all the learning I ever got. But my mother was an eddicated woman, yes'm, she could both read and write. I have the Bible she give me yit. Yes'm, you jist wait and I'll show you." After some rummaging in a box he came back with a small leather-bound Bible with print so small it was hard to read. After turning to the record of births and deaths he handed it to me, his wrinkled old face shining with pride as he said, "There, my mother wrote that with her own hand." I took the book and after a little deciphered that "Zebulon Pike Parker was born Feb. 10,

1830," written in the stiff, difficult style of long ago and written with pokeberry ink. He said his mother used to read about some "old feller that was jist covered with biles," so I read Job to him, and he was full of surprise they didn't "git some cherry bark and some sasparilly and bile it good and gin it to him."

He had a side room to
his cabin, which was
his bedroom; so that
night he spread down
a buffalo robe and
two bearskins before
the fire for Jerrine
and me. After making
sure there were
no moths in them,
I spread blankets
over them and put a
sleepy, happy little
girl to bed, for he had
insisted on making

molasses candy for her because they happened to be born on the same day of the month. And then he played the fiddle until almost one o'clock. He played all the simple, sweet, old-time pieces, in rather a squeaky, jerky way, I am afraid, but the music suited the time and the place.

Next morning he called me early and when I went out I saw such a beautiful sunrise, well worth the effort of coming to see. I had thought his cabin in a cañon, but the snow had deceived me, for a few steps from the door the mountains seemed to drop down suddenly for several hundred feet and the first of the snow

peaks seemed to
lie right at our feet.
Around its base is a
great swamp, in which
the swamp pines
grow very thickly and
from which a vapor
was rising that got
about halfway up the
snow peak all around.
Fancy to yourself a
big jewel-box of dark
green velvet lined
with silver chiffon,
the snow peak lying
like an immense opal

in its center and over all the amber light of a new day. That is what it looked most like.

Well, we next went to the corral, where I was surprised to find about thirty head of sheep. Some of them looked like they should have been sold ten years before. "Don't you ever sell any of your sheep?" I asked. "No'm. There was a feller come here once and wanted to buy some of my wethers, but I wouldn't sell any because I didn't need any money." Then he went from animal to animal, caressing each and talking to them, calling them each by name. He milked his one cow, fed his two little mules, and then we went back to the house to cook breakfast. We had delicious venison steak, smoking hot, and hoe-cakes and the "bestest" coffee, and honey.

After breakfast we set out for home. Our pack transferred to one of the little mules, we rode "Jeems," and Mr. Parker rode the other mule. He took us another way, down cañon after cañon, so that we were able to ride all the time and could make better speed. We came down out of the snow and camped within twelve miles of home in an old, deserted ranch house. We had grouse and sage chicken for supper. I was so anxious to get home that I could hardly sleep, but at last I did and was only awakened by the odor of coffee, and barely had time to wash before Zebulon Pike called breakfast. Afterwards we fixed "Jeems's" pack so that I could still ride, for Zebulon Pike was very anxious to get back to his "critters."

Poor, lonely, childlike little man! He tried to

tell me how glad he had been to entertain me. "Why," he said, "I was plumb glad to see you and right sorry to have you go. Why, I would jist as soon talk to you as to anyone. Yes'm, I would. It has been almost as good as talking to old Aunt Dilsey." If a Yankee had said the same to me I would have demanded instant apology, but I know how the Southern heart longs for dear, kindly old friends so I came on homeward, thankful for the first time that I can't talk correctly.

I got home at twelve and found, to my joy, that none of the men had returned, so I am safe from their superiority for a while, at least.

With many apologies for this outrageous letter, I am

Your ex-Washlady, Elinore Rupert.

SEDALIA AND REGALIA

November 22, 1909.
My dear Friend,—

I was dreadfully afraid that my last letter was too much for you and now I feel plumb guilty. I really don't know how to write you, for I have to write so much to say so little, and now that

my last letter made
you sick I almost
wish so many things
didn't happen to me,
for I always want
to tell you. Many
things have happened
since I last wrote,
and Zebulon Pike is
not done for by any
means, but I guess
I will tell you my
newest experience.

I am making a
wedding dress. Don't

grin; it isn't mine,—
worse luck! But I must
begin at the beginning.
Just after I wrote you
before, there came a
terrific storm which
made me appreciate
indoor coziness, but as
only Baby and I were
at home I expected
to be very lonely.
The snow was just
whirling when I saw
some one pass the
window. I opened the
door and in came the

dumpiest little woman and two daughters. She asked me if I was "Mis' Rupit." I told her that she had almost guessed it, and then she introduced herself. She said she was "Mis' Lane," that she had heard there was a new stranger in the country, so she had brought her twin girls, Sedalia and Regalia, to be neighborly. While

they were taking off
their many coats and
wraps it came out
that they were from
Linwood, thirty miles
away. I was powerful
glad I had a pot roast
and some baked
beans.

After we had put the
horses in the barn
we had dinner and I
heard the story of
the girls' odd names.
The mother is one of

those "comfy," fat little women who remain happy and bubbling with fun in spite of hard knocks. I had already fallen in love with Regalia, she is so jolly and unaffected, so fat and so plain. Sedalia has a veneer of most uncomfortable refinement. She was shocked because Gale ate all the roast she wanted, and if I had been very sensitive I would have been in tears, because I ate a helping more than Gale did.

But about the names. It seemed that "Mis' Lane" married quite young, was an orphan, and had no one to tell her things she should have known. She lived in Missouri, but about a year after her marriage the young couple started overland for the West. It was in November, and one night when they had reached the plains a real blue blizzard struck them. "Mis' Lane" had been in pain all day and soon she knew what was the matter. They were alone and it was a day's travel back to the last house. The team had given out and the wind and sleet were seeing which could do the most meanness. At last the poor man got a fire started and a wagon sheet stretched in such a manner that it kept off the sleet. He fixed a bed under the poor shelter and did all he could to keep the fire from blowing away, and there, a few hours later, a little girl baby was born. They melted sleet in the frying-pan to get water to wash it. "Mis' Lane" kept feeling no better fast, and about the time they got the poor baby dressed a second little one came.

That she told me herself is proof she didn't die, I guess, but it is right hard to believe she didn't. Luckily the fire lasted until the babies were dressed and the mother began to feel better, for there was no wood. Soon the wind stopped and the snow fell steadily. It was warmer, and the whole family snuggled up under the wagon sheet and slept.

Mr. Lane is a powerful good husband. He

waited two whole days for his wife to gain strength before he resumed the journey, and on the third morning he actually carried her to the wagon. Just think of it! Could more be asked of any man?

Every turn of the wheels made poor "Mis' Lane" more homesick. Like Mrs.

Wiggs of the Cabbage Patch, she had a taste for geographical names, and "Mis' Lane" is very loyal, so she wanted to call the little first-born "Missouri." Mr. Lane said she might, but that if she did he would call the other one "Arkansas." Sometimes homesickness would almost master her. She would hug up the little red baby and murmur "Missouri," and then daddy would growl playfully to "Arkansas." It went on that way for a long time and at last she remembered that Sedalia was in Missouri, so she felt glad and really named the older baby "Sedalia." But she could think of nothing to match the name and was in constant fear the father would name the other baby "Little Rock."

For three years poor Gale was just "t'other one." Then the Lanes went to Green River where some lodge was having a parade. They were watching the drill when a "bystander that was standing by" said something about the "fine regalia."

Instantly "Mis' Lane" thought of her unnamed child; so since that time Gale has had a name.

There could be no two people more unlike than the sisters. Sedalia is really handsome, and she is thin. But she is vain, selfish, shallow, and conceited. Gale is not even pretty, but she is clean and she is honest. She does many little things that are not exactly polite, but she is good and true. They both went to the barn with me to milk. Gale tucked up her skirts and helped me. She said, "I just love a stable, with its hay and comfortable, contented cattle. I never go into one without thinking of the little baby Christ. I almost expect to see a little red baby in the straw every time I peek into a manger."

Sedalia answered, "Well, for Heaven's sake, get out of the stable to preach. Who wants to stand among these smelly cows all day?"

They stayed with us almost a week, and one day when Gale and I were milking she asked me to invite her to stay with me a month. She said to ask her mother, and left her mother and myself much together. But Sedalia stuck to her mother like a plaster and I just could not stand Sedalia a whole month. However, I was spared all embarrassment, for "Mis' Lane" asked me if I could not find work enough to keep Gale busy for a month or two. She went on to explain that Sedalia was expecting to be married and that Gale was so "common" she would really spoil the match. I was surprised and indignant, especially as Sedalia sat and listened so brazenly, so I said I thought Sedalia would need all the help she could get to get married and that I should be glad to have Gale visit me as long as she liked.

So Gale stayed on with me. One afternoon she had gone to the post-office when I saw Mr. Patterson ride up. He went into the bunk-house to wait until the men should come. Now, from something Gale had said I fancied that Bob Patterson must be the right man. I am afraid I am not very delicate about that kind of meddling, and while I had been given to understand that Patterson was the man Sedalia expected to marry, I didn't think any man would choose her if he could get Gale, so I called him. We had a long chat and he told me frankly he wanted Gale, but that she didn't care for him, and that they kept throwing "that danged Sedalia" at him. Then he begged my pardon for saying "danged," but I told him I approved of the word when applied to Sedalia, and broke the news to him that Gale was staying with me. He fairly beamed. So that night I left Gale to wash dishes and Bob to help her while I held Mr. Stewart a prisoner in the stable and questioned him regarding Patterson's prospects and habits. I found both all that need be, and told Mr. Stewart about my talk with Patterson, and he said, "Wooman, some day ye'll gang ploom daft." But he admitted he was glad it was the "bonny lassie, instead of the bony one." When we went to the house Mr. Stewart said, "Weel, when are you douchy bairns gangin' to the kirk?"

They left it to me, so I set Thanksgiving Day, and as there is no "kirk to gang to," we are going to have a justice of the peace and they are to be

married here. We are
going to have the
dandiest dinner that
I can cook, and Mr.
Stewart went to town
next day for the
wedding dress, the
gayest plaid outside
of Caledonia. But Gale
has lots of sense
and is going to wear
it. I have it almost
finished, and while
it doesn't look just
like a Worth model,
still it looks plumb

good for me to have made. The boys are going up after Zebulon Pike, and Mr. Stewart is going after "Mis' Lane." Joy waves are radiating from this ranch and about Thanksgiving morning one will strike you.

With lots of love and happy wishes,

Your ex-Washlady,
Elinore Rupert.

A THANKSGIVING-DAY WEDDING

Dear Mrs. Coney,—

... I think every one enjoyed our Thanksgiving programme except poor Gale. She was grieved, I verily believe, because Mr. Patterson is not Mormon and could not take Sedalia and herself also. I suppose it seemed odd to her to be unable to give way to Sedalia as she had always done.

I had cooked and cooked. Gale and Zebulon Pike both helped all they could. The wedding was to be at twelve o'clock, so at ten I hustled Gale into my room to dress. I had to lock the door to keep her in, and I divided my time between the last touches to my dinner and the finishing touches to Gale's toilet and receiving the people. The Lane party had not come yet, and I was scared to death lest Sedalia had had a tantrum and that Mr. Stewart would not get back in time. At last I left the people to take care of themselves, for I had too much on my mind to bother with them. Just after eleven Mr. Stewart, Mis' Lane, Sedalia, and Pa Lane "arriv" and came at once into the kitchen to warm. In a little while poor, frightened Gale came creeping in, looking guilty. But she looked lovely, too, in spite of her plaid dress. She wore her hair in a coronet braid, which added dignity and height, as well as being simple and becoming. Her mother brought her a wreath for her hair, of lilies of the valley and tiny pink rosebuds. It might seem a little out of place to one who didn't see it, but the effect was really charming.

Sedalia didn't know that Mr. Stewart had given Gale her dress, so, just to be nasty, she said, as soon as she saw Gale, "Dear me, when are you going to dress, Gale? You will hardly have time to get out of that horse-blanket you are wearing and get into something decent." You see, she thought it was one of my dresses fixed over for Gale. Presently Sedalia asked me if I was invited to the "function." She had some kind of rash on her face and Zebulon Pike noticed the rash and heard the word "function," so he thought that was the name of some disease and asked Mr. Stewart if the "function" was "catching." Mr. Stewart had heard Sedalia, but knew "Zebbie" had not heard all that was said and how he got the idea he had, so he answered, "Yes, if ye once get the fever." So Zebulon Pike privately warned every one against getting the "function" from Sedalia. There are plenty of people here who don't know exactly what a function is, myself among them. So people edged away from Sedalia, and some asked her if she had seen the doctor and what he thought of her case. Poor girl, I'm afraid she didn't have a very enjoyable time.

At last the "jestice"

of the peace came, and I hope they live happy ever afterward. That night a dance was given to celebrate the event and we began to have dinner immediately after the wedding so as to get through in time to start, for dances are never given in the home here, but in "the hall." Every settlement has one and the invitations are merely written announcements posted everywhere. We have what Sedalia calls "homogenous" crowds. I wouldn't attempt to say what she means, but as everybody goes no doubt she is right.

Our dinner was a success, but that is not to be wondered at. Every woman for miles around contributed. Of course we had to borrow dishes, but we couldn't think of seating every one; so we set one table for twenty-four and had three other long tables, on one of which we placed all the meats, pickles, and sauces, on another the vegetables, soup, and coffee, and on the third the pie, cakes, ice-cream, and other desserts. We had two big, long shelves, one above the other, on which were the dishes. The people helped themselves to dishes and neighbors took turns at serving from the tables, so people got what they wanted and hunted themselves a place to sit while they ate. Two of the cowboys from this ranch waited upon the table at which were the wedding party and some of their friends. Boys from other ranches helped serve and carried coffee, cake, and ice-cream. The tablecloths were tolerably good linen and we had ironed them wet so they looked nice. We had white lace-paper on the shelves and we used drawn-work paper napkins. As I said, we borrowed dishes, or, that is, every woman who called herself our neighbor brought whatever she thought we would need. So after every one had eaten I suggested that they sort out their dishes and wash them, and in that way I was saved all that work. We had everything done and were off to the dance by five o'clock. We went in sleds and sleighs, the snow was so deep, but it was all so jolly. Zebbie, Mr. Stewart, Jerrine, and I went in the bobsled. We jogged along at a comfortable pace lest the "beasties" should suffer, and every now and then a merry party would fly past us scattering snow in our faces and yelling like Comanches. We had a lovely moon then and the snow was so beautiful! We were driving northward, and to the south and back of us were the great somber, pine-clad Uintah Mountains, while ahead and on every side were the bare buttes, looking like old men of the mountains,—so old they had lost all their hair, beard, and teeth.

ZEBULON PIKE VISITS HIS OLD HOME

December 28, 1909.
Dear Mrs. Coney,—

Our Thanksgiving affair was the most enjoyable happening I can remember for a long time. Zebulon Pike came, but I had as a bait for him two fat letters from home. As soon as I came back from his place I wrote to Mrs. Carter and trusted to luck for my letter to reach her. I told her all I could about her brother and how seldom he left his mountain home. I asked her to write him all she could in one letter, as the trips between our place and his were so few and far between. So when she received

my letter she wrote
all she could think
of, and then sent her
letter and mine to
Mothie and Phœbe,
who are widows
living in the old
home. They each
took turns writing,
so their letters
are a complete
record of the years
"Zebbie" has been
gone. The letters
were addressed to
me along with a

cordial letter from Mrs. Carter asking me to see that he got them and to use my judgment in the delivering. I couldn't go myself, but I wanted to read the letters to him and to write the answers; so I selected one piece of news I felt would bring him to hear the rest without his knowing how much there was for him.

Well, the boys brought him, and a more delighted little man I am sure never lived. I read the letters over and over, and answers were hurried off. He was dreadfully homesick, but couldn't figure on how he could leave the "critters," or how he could trust himself on a train. Mr. Stewart became interested, and he is a very resourceful man, so an old Frenchman was found who had no home and wanted a place to stay so he could trap. He was installed at Zebulon Pike's with full instructions as to each "critter's" peculiarities and needs. Then one of the boys, who was going home for Christmas to Memphis, was induced to wait for Mr. Parker and to see him safe to Little Rock. His money was banked for him, and Mr. Stewart saw that he was properly clothed and made comfortable for the trip. Then he sent a telegram to Judge Carter, who met Zebulon Pike at Little Rock, and they had a family reunion in Yell County. I have had some charming letters from there, but that only proves what I have always said, that I am the luckiest woman in finding really lovely people and having really happy experiences. Good things are constantly happening to me. I wish I could tell you about my happy Christmas, but one of my New Year's resolutions

was to stop loading
you down with
two-thousand-word
letters.

From something
you wrote I think I
must have written
boastingly to you at
some time. I have
certainly not intended
to, and you must
please forgive me
and remember how
ignorant I am and
how hard it is for me

to express myself properly. I felt after I had written to Mr. Parker's people that I had taken a liberty, but luckily it was not thought of in that way by them. If you only knew how far short I fall of my own hopes you would know I could never boast. Why, it keeps me busy making over mistakes just like some one using old clothes. I get myself all ready to enjoy a success and find that I have to fit a failure. But one consolation is that I generally have plenty of material to cut generously, and many of my failures have proved to be real blessings.

I do hope this New Year may bring to you the desire of your heart and all that those who love you best most wish for you.

With lots and lots of love from baby and myself.

Your ex-washlady, Elinore Rupert.

A HAPPY CHRISTMAS

Dear Mrs. Coney,—

My happy Christmas
resulted from
the ex-sheriff of
this county being
snowbound here. It
seems that persons
who come from a
lower altitude to this
country frequently
become bewildered,
especially if in poor

health, leave the train at any stop and wander off into the hills, sometimes dying before they are found. The ex-sheriff cited a case, that of a young German who was returning from the Philippines, where he had been discharged after the war. He was the only child of his widowed mother, who has a ranch a few miles from here.

No one knew he was coming home. One day the cook belonging to the camp of a construction gang went hunting and came back running, wild with horror. He had found the body of a man. The coroner and the sheriff were notified, and next morning went out for the body, but the wolves had almost destroyed it. High up in a willow, under which the poor man had lain down to die, they saw a small bundle tied in a red bandanna and fast to a branch. They found a letter addressed to whoever should find it, saying that the body was that of Benny Louderer and giving them directions how to spare his poor old mother the awful knowledge of how he died. Also there was a letter to his mother asking her not to grieve for him and to keep their days faithfully. "Their days," I afterward learned, were anniversaries which they had always kept, to which was added "Benny's day."

Poor boy! When he realized that death was near his every

thought was for the mother. Well, they followed his wishes, and the casket containing the bare, gnawed bones was sealed and never opened. And to this day poor Mrs. Louderer thinks her boy died of some fever while yet aboard the transport. The manner of his death has been kept so secret that I am the only one who has heard it.

I was so sorry for the poor mother that I resolved to visit her the first opportunity I had. I am at liberty to go where I please when there is no one to cook for. So, when the men left, a few days later, I took Jerrine and rode over to the Louderer ranch. I had never

seen Mrs. Louderer
and it happened to be
"Benny's day" that I
blundered in upon. I
found her to be a dear
old German woman
living all alone, the
people who do the
work on the ranch
living in another house
two miles away. She
had been weeping
for hours when I
got there, but in
accordance with her
custom on the many

anniversaries, she had a real feast prepared, although no one had been bidden.

She says that God always sends her guests, but that was the first time she had had a little girl. She had a little daughter once herself, little Gretchen, but all that was left was a sweet memory and a pitifully small mound on the ranch, quite near the house, where Benny and Gretchen are at rest beside "der fader, Herr Louderer."

She is such a dear old lady! She made us so welcome and she is so entertaining. All the remainder of the day we listened to stories of her children, looked at her pictures, and Jerrine had a lovely time with a wonderful wooden doll that they had brought with them from Germany. Mrs. Louderer forgot to weep in recalling her childhood days and showing us her treasures. And then our feast,—for it was verily a feast. We had goose and it was so delicious. I couldn't tell you half the good things any more than I could have eaten some of all of them.

We sat talking until far into the night, and she asked me how I was going to spend Christmas. I told her, "Probably in being homesick." She said that would never do and suggested that we spend it together. She said it was one of their special days and that the only happiness left her

was in making some
one else happy; so
she had thought of
cooking some nice
things and going to as
many sheep camps as
she could, taking with
her the good things
to the poor exiles,
the sheep-herders.
I liked the plan and
was glad to agree,
but I never dreamed
I should have so
lovely a time. When
the queer old wooden

clock announced two
we went to bed.

I left quite early the
next morning with my
head full of Christmas
plans. You may not
know, but cattle-men
and sheep-men
cordially hate each
other. Mr. Stewart
is a cattle-man, and
so I didn't mention
my Christmas plans
to him. I saved all
the butter I could

spare for the sheep-
herders; they never
have any. That
and some jars of
gooseberry jelly was
all I could give them.
I cooked plenty for
the people here,
and two days before
Christmas I had a
chance to go down to
Mrs. Louderer's in a
buggy, so we went.
We found her up to
her ears in cooking,
and such sights and

smells I could never describe. She was so glad I came early, for she needed help. I never worked so hard in my life or had a pleasanter time.

Mrs. Louderer had sent a man out several days before to find out how many camps there were and where they were located. There were twelve camps and that means twenty-four men. We roasted six geese, boiled three small hams and three hens. We had besides several meat-loaves and links of sausage. We had twelve large loaves of the best rye bread; a small tub of doughnuts; twelve coffee-cakes, more to be called fruit-cakes, and also a quantity of little cakes with seeds, nuts, and fruit in them,—so pretty to look at and so good to taste. These had a thick coat of icing, some brown, some pink, some white. I had thirteen pounds of butter and six pint jars of jelly, so we melted the jelly and poured it into twelve glasses.

The plan was, to start real early Christmas

Eve morning, make our circuit of camps, and wind up the day at Frau O'Shaughnessy's to spend the night. Yes, Mrs. O'Shaughnessy is Irish,—as Irish as the pigs in Dublin. Before it was day the man came to feed and to get our horses ready. We were up betimes and had breakfast. The last speck was wiped from the shining stove, the kitchen floor was scrubbed, and the last small thing put in order. The man had four horses harnessed and hitched to the sled, on which was placed a wagon-box filled with straw, hot rocks, and blankets. Our twelve apostles— that is what we called our twelve boxes— were lifted in and tied firmly into place. Then we clambered in and away we went. Mrs. Louderer drove, and Tam O'Shanter and Paul Revere were snails compared to us. We didn't follow any road either, but went sweeping along across country. No one else in the world could have done it unless they were drunk. We went careening along hill-sides without even slacking the trot. Occasionally we struck a particularly stubborn bunch of sagebrush and even the sled-runners would jump up into the air. We didn't stop to light, but hit the earth several feet in advance of where we left it. Luck was with us, though. I hardly expected to get through with my head unbroken, but not even a glass was cracked.

It would have done your heart good to see the sheep-men. They were all delighted, and when you consider that they live solely on canned corn and tomatoes, beans, salt pork, and coffee, you can fancy what they thought of their treat. They have mutton when it is fit to eat, but that is certainly not in winter. One man at each camp does the cooking and the other herds. It doesn't make any difference if the cook never cooked before, and most of them never did. At one camp, where we stopped for dinner, they had a most interesting collection of fossils. After delivering our last "apostle," we turned our faces toward Frau O'Shaughnessy's, and got there just in time for supper.

Mrs. O'Shaughnessy is a widow, too, and has quite an interesting story. She is a dumpy little woman whose small nose seems to be smelling the stars, it is so tip-tilted. She has the merriest blue eyes and the quickest wit. It is really worth a severe bumping just to be welcomed by her.

It was so warm and cozy in her low little cabin. She had her table set for supper, but she laid plates for us and put before us a beautifully roasted chicken. Thrifty Mrs. Louderer thought it should have been saved until next day, so she said to Frau

O'Shaughnessy, "We hate to eat your hen, best you save her till tomorrow." But Mrs. O'Shaughnessy answered, "Oh, 't is no mather, 't is an ould hin she was annyway." So we enjoyed the "ould hin," which was brown, juicy, and tender.

When we had finished supper and were

drinking our "tay," Mrs. O'Shaughnessy told our fortunes with the tea-leaves. She told mine first and said I would die an old maid. I said it was rather late for that, but she cheerfully replied, "Oh, well, better late than niver." She predicted for Mrs. Louderer that she should shortly catch a beau. "'T is the next man you see that will come coortin' you." Before we left the table some one knocked and a young man, a sheep-herder, entered. He belonged to a camp a few miles away and is out from Boston in search of health. He had been into town and his horse was lamed so he could not make it into camp, and he wanted to stay overnight. He was a stranger to us all, but Mrs. O'Shaughnessy made him at home and fixed such a tempting supper for him that I am sure he was glad of the chance to stay. He was very decidedly English, and powerfully proud of it. He asked Mrs. O'Shaughnessy if she was Irish and she said, "No, ye haythen, it's Chinese Oi am.

Can't yez tell it be me Cockney accint?" Mr. Boutwell looked very much surprised. I don't know which was the funnier, the way he looked or what she said.

We had a late breakfast Christmas morning, but before we were through Mr. Stewart came. We had planned to spend the day with

Mrs. O'Shaughnessy, but he didn't approve of our going into the sheep district, so when he found where we had gone he came after us. Mrs. Louderer and he are old acquaintances and he bosses her around like he tries to boss me. Before we left, Mrs. O'Shaughnessy's married daughter came, so we knew she would not be lonely.

It was almost one o'clock when we got home, but all hands helped and I had plenty cooked anyway, so we soon had a good dinner on the table. Mr. Stewart had prepared a Christmas box for Jerrine and me. He doesn't approve of white waists in the winter. I had worn one at the wedding and he felt personally aggrieved. For me in the box were two dresses, that is, the material to make them. One is a brown and red checked, and the other green with a white fleck in, both outing flannel. For Jerrine there was a pair of shoes and stockings, both stockings full of candy and nuts. He is very bluff in manner, but he is really the kindest person.

Mrs. Louderer stayed until New Year's day. My Christmas was really a very happy one.

Your friend,
Elinore Rupert.

... An interesting day on this ranch is the day the cattle are named. If Mr. Stewart

had children he would
as soon think of
leaving them unnamed
as to let a "beastie"
go without a name.

On the day they
vaccinated he came
into the kitchen and
told me he would need
me to help him name
the "critters." So he
and I "assembled"
in a safe place and
took turns naming the
calves. As fast as a

calf was vaccinated it was run out of the chute and he or I called out a name for it and it was booked that way.

The first two he named were the "Duke of Monmouth" and the "Duke of Montrose." I called my first "Oliver Cromwell" and "John Fox." The poor "mon" had to have revenge, so the next ugly, scrawny little beast he called the "Poop of Roome." And it was a heifer calf, too.

This morning I had the startling news that the "Poop" had eaten too much alfalfa and was all "swellit oop," and, moreover, he had "stealit it." I don't know which is the more astonishing, that the Pope has stolen alfalfa, or that he has eaten it.

We have a swell lot of names, but I am not sure I could tell you which is "Bloody Mary," or which is "Elizabeth," or, indeed, which is which of any of them.

E.R.

A CONFESSION

April 5, 1910.
Dear Mrs. Coney,—

I find upon re-reading your letter that I did not answer it at all when I wrote you. You must think me very indifferent, but I really don't mean to be.

My house joins on to

Mr. Stewart's house. It was built that way so that I could "hold down" my land and job at the same time. I see the wisdom of it now, though at first I did not want it that way. My boundary lines run within two feet of Mr. Stewart's house, so it was quite easy to build on.

I think the Pattersons' ranch

is about twenty-five miles from us. I am glad to tell you they are doing splendidly. Gale is just as thrifty as she can be and Bobby is steady and making money fast. Their baby is the dearest little thing. I have heard that Sedalia is to marry a Mormon bishop, but I doubt it. She puts on very disgusting airs about "our Bobby,"

and she patronizes
Gale most shamefully;
but Gale, bless her
unconscious heart,
is so happy in her
husband and son that
she doesn't know
Sedalia is insulting.

My dear old
grandmother whom
I loved so much
has gone home to
God. I used to write
long letters to her.
I should like a few

addresses of old persons who are lonely as she was, who would like letters such as I write. You know I can't be brief. I have tried and cannot. If you know of any persons who would not tire of my long accounts and would care to have them, you will be doing me a favor to let me know.

I have not treated you

quite frankly about
something you had a
right to know about.
I am ashamed and
I regret very much
that I have not told
you. I so dread the
possibility of losing
your friendship that
I will never tell you
unless you promise
me beforehand to
forgive me. I know
that is unfair, but it
is the only way I can
see out of a difficulty

that my foolish reticence has led me into. Few people, perhaps, consider me reticent, but in some cases I am afraid I am even deceitful. Won't you make it easy to "'fess" so I may be happy again?

Truly your friend,
Elinore Rupert.

June 16, 1910.
My Dear Friend,—

Your card just to
hand. I wrote you
some time ago telling
you I had a confession
to make and have
had no letter since,
so thought perhaps
you were scared I had
done something too
bad to forgive. I am
suffering just now
from eye-strain and
can't see to write

long at a time, but I reckon I had better confess and get it done with.

The thing I have done is to marry Mr. Stewart. It was such an inconsistent thing to do that I was ashamed to tell you. And, too, I was afraid you would think I didn't need your friendship and might desert me. Another

of my friends thinks
that way.

I hope my eyes will
be better soon and
then I will write you a
long letter.

Your old friend with a
new name,

Elinore Stewart.

ABOUT THE AUTHOR

Elinore Pruitt Stewart was born on June 3rd, 1876 in White Bead Hill, which was then a settlement in Chickasaw Nation, Indian Territory, and is now in Oklahoma. She offers a window into her bold life with these adventurous letters, which were the basis for the 1979 film Heartland.

ABOUT THE COVER

The cover is adapted from an Untitled Pastoral Scene by the American painter, David Johnson from 1867.

MORE BOOKS AT:
superlargeprint.com

KEEP ON READING!

This book is set in a font designed by
Abelardo Gonzalez called OpenDyslexic.

ISBN 1548606553
ISBN 978-1548606558

Made in the USA
Coppell, TX
31 January 2020

15226880R00134